LIONS

Written and edited by **Lucy Baker**

Consultant Douglas M Richardson, Head Keeper
Lion Terraces, London Zoo

TWO-CAN

First published in Great Britain in 1991 by
Two-Can Publishing Ltd
346 Old Street
London EC1V 9NQ

British Library Cataloguing in Publication Data
Baker, Lucy
Lions.
1. Lions
I. Title
599.74428

ISBN 1-85434-094-8

Photographic Credits:
Front Cover Clem Haagner/Ardea p.4 John Shaw/NHPA p.5 Peter Johnson/NHPA p.6-7 Matthews/Purdy/Survival Anglia p.8 Matthews/Purdy/Survival Anglia p.9 Jen &
Des Bartlett/Bruce Coleman Ltd p.10-11 Matthews/Purdy/Survival Anglia p.13 G. Zeisler/Bruce Coleman Ltd p.14 Matthews/Purdy/Survival Anglia p.15 Philip Perry/Frank
Lane Picture Agency p.16 Matthews/Purdy/Survival Anglia p.17 (top) John Cancalosi/Bruce Coleman Ltd (bottom) Richard Waller/Ardea p.18 Jen & Des Bartlett/Survival
Anglia p.19 Y. Arthus-Bertrand/Ardea.

Illustration Credits:
Back Cover p.4-19 David Cook/Linden Artists p.20-21 Steve Ling/Linden Artists p.22-23 Claire Legemah p.24-25 Ken Hooks/Jeremy Clegg p.26-30 Alan Male/Linden
Artists p.31 Alan Rogers

CONTENTS

LOOKING AT LIONS

Lions are members of the big cat family. Their closest relatives are tigers, leopards and jaguars. Most big cats have spots or stripes on their fur coats, but lions are a plain, sandy-yellow colour.

For many centuries lions have been known as the King of Beasts. Although they are not as big as some tigers, male lions have a ring of long hair around their head, neck and shoulders called a mane. This mane gives them a very majestic appearance.

Lions once roamed over much of Europe, Africa and the Middle East. Today most lions can be found on rich grasslands or desert sands in parts of Africa. India has a tiny lion population living in an area of protected forest.

▲ Female lions are also called lionesses. They are smaller and lighter than male lions, and they do not have manes. The female in this picture is licking her paws clean with her rough tongue. This is called grooming. Lions are often seen grooming themselves and each other.

▶ A handsome male lion shows off his mane. The ring of long hair around his head, neck and shoulders makes the lion look bigger than he really is.

LION FACTS

The largest lions measure over three metres (about 10 feet) from the tips of their noses to the ends of their tails.

Lions have a tuft of long, black hair at the ends of their tails. Sometimes, lions use their tufted tails to brush off flies and other biting insects.

LIFE IN THE PRIDE

Most members of the cat family lead solitary and secretive lives, but lions live in groups called prides. There can be over 30 lions in a large pride.

Lion prides are rather like human families, but the mix of adults is different. The main members of the pride are a number of related females and their young. A smaller number of males complete the group. The males are not related to the females, but they are likely to be related to each other.

Male lions are not permanent members of a pride. At any time, they may be forced to leave their pride by rival males. Old or weak lions may be killed during fierce battles.

The female lions in a pride live as equals. They share the daily tasks of motherhood, hunting and deciding the group's movements. The males spend most of their time defending the pride's territory and looking for mates.

All the lions within a pride are friends. When they meet each other, they rub heads in greeting. The females spend their free time playing with the cubs or each other.

It is rare to see a whole lion pride. The lions usually split into smaller groups. At dawn and dusk, they communicate over long distances by making deep, throaty roars. Lions also roar to warn off neighbouring prides.

MAKING BABIES

Lions do not mate at a particular time of year. Instead, the females become ready to mate every few weeks or months.

Often all the females in a pride are ready to mate at the same time. They make a steady rumbling noise and produce a strong scent, which attracts the male lions. Each female teams up with a male from her pride.

Females remain ready for two to five days. During that time the males will mate with them frequently. And yet the females are unlikely to become pregnant. People who have studied lions in the wild estimate that mating has to take place over 1,000 times to produce a single litter of cubs.

Once a female lion becomes pregnant she will not mate again for nearly two years, unless her cubs die. About 15 weeks after her pregnancy begins, she gives birth to a litter of tiny, helpless cubs.

Most lion litters contain two to four cubs. The cubs are hidden in thick undergrowth for the first few weeks of life. Every few days their mother carries them to a new hiding place to prevent other animals tracking them and attacking them.

When rival males take over a lion pride they sometimes eat the newborn cubs. This behaviour is not fully understood, but the male lions probably kill the cubs so that the females in the pride will mate with them again.

► These lions have just finished mating. The male lion must get away from the female quickly. She will snarl or swat at him if he takes too long.

◄ Male lions usually keep their distance from the females in their pride. When they are mating, they stay with their partners and follow them wherever they go.

CUB FACTS

Lion cubs are only about 30 cm (12 inches) long at birth. They are blind, helpless and tiny.

Cubs have spots on their coats when they are born.

Lion cubs are carried in their mothers' mouths during the first weeks of their lives.

GROWING UP

When lion cubs are six weeks old, they are led out to meet the rest of their pride. All the lions are friendly toward the cubs. Any females that are producing milk let the new cubs feed from their breasts.

Lion cubs suckle milk until they are six months old. During that time they are slowly introduced to a meat diet.

Very few lion cubs survive the first three years of their life. Young females that live this long are usually allowed to stay in the pride. Young males have to leave. Three-year-old males are as big as their mothers, and are a threat to the adult males in the pride.

Young lions that leave their prides have to live alone or in small groups. It is more difficult to survive without the pride's support.

◀ Lion cubs are very affectionate. They often rub up against the adults or sleep by their side.

▼ Lion cubs play like kittens. They often wrestle with each other or chase an adult lion's tail.

GROWING FACTS

Unlike their parents, lion cubs have lightly spotted coats and short, tapering tails for the first few months of their lives.

Male lion cubs develop manes when they are two to three years old.

ON THE HUNT

Lions are expert hunters. They specialise in catching, killing and eating animals. The list of animals that they catch includes zebras, wildebeest and antelopes.

Large prey such as buffalo and giraffe may be caught by a group of hunting lions. Desert lions include the small, prickly porcupine in their diet.

Almost all of a lion pride's food is caught by the females. To track their prey down, lions go out alone or in small groups. When they see possible victims, they approach the animals with care.

Lions have to get quite close to their prey before they stand a chance of catching them. Almost all their victims can outrun them over long distances. Lions stalk their prey by moving slowly and quietly through the undergrowth, and freezing whenever the animals look up.

Lions hunting in a group work together. They spread out over a short distance and try to trap animals between them. Even so, only one out of every five attempts to catch food is successful.

As well as catching their own food, lions will scavenge on dead and dying animals. They watch vultures to locate rich pickings. Lions will also rob hyenas and cheetahs of their kill.

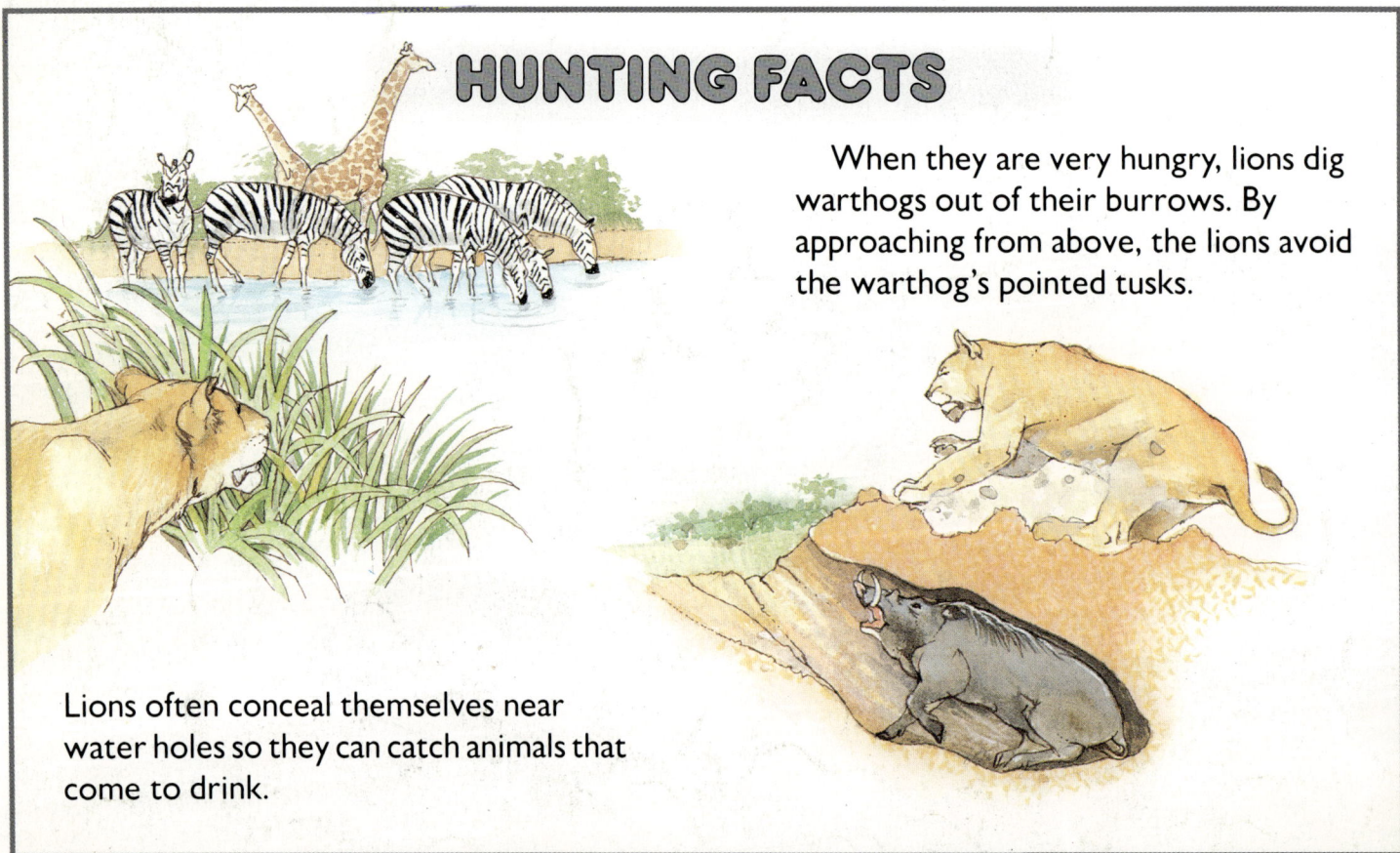

HUNTING FACTS

When they are very hungry, lions dig warthogs out of their burrows. By approaching from above, the lions avoid the warthog's pointed tusks.

Lions often conceal themselves near water holes so they can catch animals that come to drink.

▲ When lions get close to their prey, they sprint after them. Lions can run very fast over a short distance, but their prey can outrun them over long distances. This zebra can outrun the lion if it is not caught quickly.

▼ A lion's prey is killed in different ways. Sometimes the animal's throat is bitten. Other times, its mouth is clamped shut by the lion's huge jaws. Lions use their long, sharply pointed teeth to kill their prey.

MEAL TIMES

Once an animal has been caught and killed by one lion, other members of the pride may feast on the carcass.

If there is a lot of food, all the lions get their share. If there is not enough to go round, the lions squabble over the meal. Plundering takes place at all levels. Female lions will steal food from cubs, and male lions will steal food from female lions.

Lions need over five kilograms (11 pounds) of meat a day. Often they eat much more than this in one sitting and then rest for a few days. They can eat over 25 kg (55 pounds) of meat in one go. Lions have uncomfortable, swollen bellies after a big meal.

Lions remove the stomach of their victim, drag it a short distance and rake it over with grass, sticks and dirt. Nobody knows why. Skin and bones are not eaten unless the lions are extremely hungry.

Pieces of the kill may be taken away by individual lions or the whole carcass may be dragged into the shade. A large carcass is sometimes guarded so that the pride can feast on it again.

To deter other lions from its kill, a lion draws back its lips, narrows its eyes and makes a snarling or hissing noise.

Lions sometimes graze like cows on large grass blades.

When lions are eating alone, packs of hyenas may steal their food.

▲ Lions drink like domestic cats, by lapping at the water's surface with their tongues. Desert lions can survive without water for up to a month, but most lions drink once a day.

◄ Male lions that live within a pride rarely catch their own food. They take from the females' kills. People call the biggest slice of cake or the largest portion of ice cream the lion's share because male lions take what they want from a pride's kill.

TIME OFF

Lions sleep up to 20 hours a day. While the sun blazes in the sky, most lions snooze in a cool or shady spot. Some lions lie in dry river beds or damp sand banks. Others sleep in shady thickets or up a tree.

Lions are most active at dawn and dusk. As the sun drops from the sky and the air cools, they stir themselves for a night's hunting. Their task is made easier by the fading light. Pride males often choose this time to patrol their territory, searching for intruders.

As the sun rises, lions finish the remains of the night's kill or drink at a local water hole. Some lions may roar, to communicate with other members of their pride or warn off intruders.

By the time the long hot day has begun, lions are most likely to be back in their resting places, stretching, yawning and preparing for another long sleep.

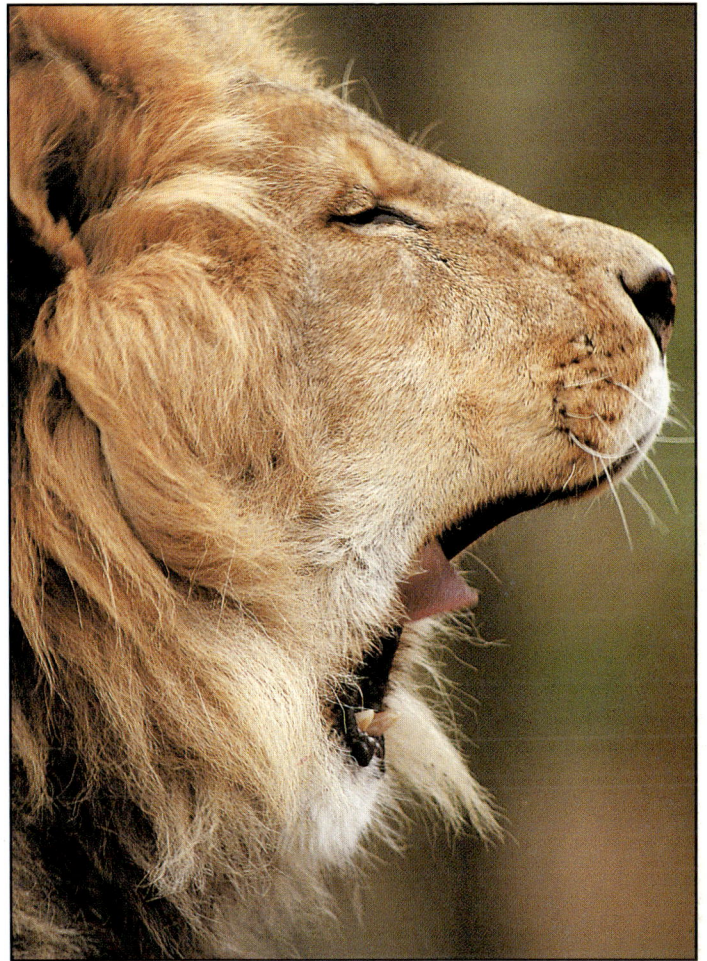

▲ It is quite common to see a lion yawning. When one lion yawns, the lions that are lying nearby often begin yawning too.

◄ Sometimes lions sleep on their backs with their bellies in the air. The fur on their bellies is longer, softer and whiter than the rest of their coat.

► If there are suitable trees in their area, lions can often be found sleeping high in the branches. There is a cool breeze at this level, and fewer biting flies. However, because lions are such big cats they need very large trees to get comfortable in the branches. Usually lions are seen sleeping in the shade of a tree rather than in its boughs.

LIONS AND PEOPLE

Lions once had a reputation for eating people. Now it is thought that few lions would actually attack a human.

Most killer lions have turned out to be old or injured animals that eat people because they can no longer catch their usual prey. However, there are some notorious cases. In Kenya, two healthy lions were shot because they caught and ate the workmen who were trying to build a railway line through their territory.

Many centuries ago, the Roman emperors used lions as executioners. They kept them in dens and fed them the criminals of the day. The practice was continued until medieval times in central and southern Europe.

▼ Lions were once big game. Now people are more likely to shoot them with tranquiliser darts than bullets. Lions are put to sleep so that they can be examined by gamekeepers and scientists. Some lions are fitted with radio collars so that their movements can be studied.

▲ A few lion cubs have been reared by hand. Far from being a threat to humans, lions that have grown up with people can become quite tame.

Today, most lions are afraid of people. They have been hunted in great numbers for sport, and killed for eating farmers' livestock. Their numbers are greatly reduced.

The vast majority of surviving lions live within the confines of national parks. Here they are protected from hunters, and people and livestock are protected from them.

LIONS FACTS

Lions are often used as symbols of strength and courage. They appear on coats of arms, flags and shields. Lion statues are added to large buildings to make them look more impressive.

GRASSLANDS GAME

Can you help the lion cub find her pride? She has got lost in the long grass. You will need a dice and some counters to play this game.

BE CAREFUL – if you land on a black square you have to start again.

START

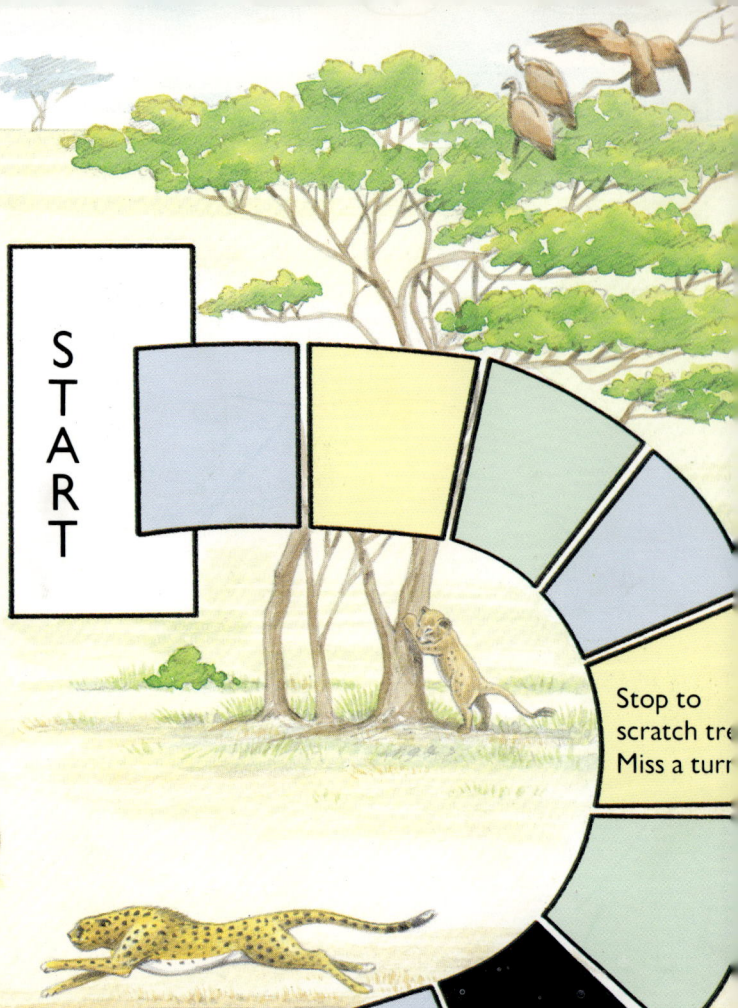

Stop to scratch tre Miss a turn

Hurry to avoid cheetah. Forward 2 spaces.

Take short cut through the thicket.

Stop to rest. Miss a turn.

Chase porcupine. Miss a turn.

Hide fro hyenas. Th again.

Spot a member of the pride. Hurry on 4 spaces.

Stop to drink. Miss a turn.

Chase ranger's car and lose direction. Miss a turn.

Pick up scent of pride. Throw again.

Wait for wildebeest to pass. Miss a turn.

FINISH

LION MASK

Try making a mask. You will need a piece of cardboard or thick paper, a length of elastic or string and a pair of scissors.

Draw the basic mask shape on to the cardboard. Remember to make two holes for your eyes and a small hole at each side of the mask. Carefully cut out your mask shape and then decide how you are going to decorate it. When your mask is decorated, thread the elastic or string through the two holes at the side. Now your mask is ready to wear.

There are lots of ways to decorate masks. Here are a few things to try.

crayons

wool

paint

coloured paper

fabric

▶ Our mask was made by cutting out the basic shapes from cardboard and sticking them together as shown.

FIND THE LIONS

There are six lions hiding in this picture.
Can you find them?

There is one more animal in the picture.
Do you know its name?

A PRIDE OF THEIR OWN

BY LUCY BAKER

Caspar and Sebastian were brothers. They grew up on the African plains.

For the first few weeks of their lives, Caspar and Sebastian had been helpless cubs. Their mother had hidden them in thick undergrowth. She fed them and carried them from one place of shelter to another.

Caspar's earliest memories were his happiest ones. He remembered the first time he and Sebastian ventured out on wobbly legs. They had stumbled down to a small water hole and peered in.

Caspar had been fascinated but a little frightened by what he saw: two wide-eyed cubs with spotty faces and large ears. He had not realised that it was a reflection until his brother had pointed it out.

When their mother had led them out of their hiding place to meet the pride, Caspar had marvelled at all the new friends he had. Not just other cubs, but big adult lions that would let him play on their backs or chase their tails.

Sebastian's favourite memories were different. He liked to recall the

hunting lessons. When they were four months old, Caspar and Sebastian had been allowed to join their mother's hunting party for the first time.

It had been a cool, dark night. The air was filled with excitement. All around, members of their pride had groaned and roared as hunger gnawed at their bellies. Sebastian had tried to roar too, but had only managed a pitiful mewing.

For a long time, the group had moved quietly through the long grass. Every lion had been scanning the horizon for a possible meal. Then, at last, a herd of wildebeest had come into sight.

Crouching low in the scrubby grass, the lions had closed in around the herd. Sebastian and Caspar had been told to stay quiet and still, to watch the other lions hunt.

Quick as a flash, the adult lions had lifted their heads and begun to sprint towards their prey. They moved so fast that it was difficult to follow what happened. Two of the wildebeest were trapped completely and brought down by the weight of pouncing lions. The rest of the herd scattered.

It was a wonderful feast. Their mother had carefully torn off a small piece of meat for the cubs to chew on, and when they had finished, she cleaned their faces with her big, rough tongue.

Life was easy for Caspar and Sebastian throughout their early years. Long, lazy days led on to nights of hunting practice and play. But slowly, things began to change.

By the time the brothers were three years old, they had outgrown their mother and the other female lions. The adult males in the pride gave them a wide berth and growled when they approached. It was time for the brothers to leave.

Sebastian was keen to go, to grow up and become like the father-figures in his pride. Caspar was reluctant. It was not until one of the adult males bit him on the nose that Caspar was persuaded to join his brother.

The brothers stayed close together. They liked each other's company in the long, lazy days, and hunting was easier with both of them taking part.

For three years they wandered across the savannah and bushlands. They saw elephants push over trees with their powerful trunks. When it rained, they sheltered under tall trees while families of giraffes munched on the high leaves. During the dry season, when the grass became parched and golden yellow, they made long detours to the busy water holes.

With the two of them hunting, Caspar and Sebastian managed to catch enough food, but both knew there was something wrong. They were always on the move, forced on by the territorial roars of local prides. What they really wanted to do was settle down and live the lives their fathers had enjoyed. It was time to find a pride of their own.

Young and bold, they tried to take the very next pride they came across. Ignoring the warning calls of the resident males, they strode into the forbidden territory and began to flirt with the females they met.

Within hours of their arrival, the resident males had appeared in force. Sebastian and Caspar had picked foolishly. The pride they were after had four resident males. The brothers were outnumbered by angry lions.

After a short and painful fight, the two brothers fled back to the open plains. They were disappointed by their defeat, and groaned and roared as they nursed their wounds and scratches.

It took several months before they were strong enough to try again. This time they chose a smaller pride. It was a good choice. The two resident males were old and unhealthy. The fight was over quickly. The old lions staggered off bleeding and tired, while Caspar and Sebastian suffered barely a scratch.

The females of the pride were wary of the brothers at first, but soon they were rubbing up against them.

Caspar and Sebastian were filled with joy. They had claimed their rightful place in the world. They looked out on the open plains they had wandered for so long, and roared with pleasure. They had found home.

TRUE OR FALSE?

Which of these facts are true and which ones are false? If you have read this book carefully you will know the answers.

1. The lion is known as the King of Beasts.

2. Today, most lions live in African national parks.
3. There are more males than females in a lion pride.
4. Lions have long, bushy tails.
5. Baby lions are called kittens.
6. Male lions do most of the hunting for the pride.
7. Female lions are also called lionesses.
8. Lions are most active during the daytime.
9. The ring of long hair around a male lion's head is called a mane.

10. Packs of hyenas may steal food from individual lions.
11. Lions sometimes chew grass.
12. Lions can run faster than their prey over long distances.
13. Lions drink by lapping at the water with their tongues.
14. Lions sometimes sleep up trees.

15. In Roman times, people were thrown to the lions if they disobeyed the emperor.

INDEX

For more information about TWO-CAN books, write to TWO-CAN Publishing, 346 Old Street, London, EC1V 9NQ.